CHESAPEAKE

A BOOK OF 21 POSTCARDS

BROWNTROUT PUBLISHERS
SAN FRANCISCO • CALIFORNIA

BROWNTROUT PUBLISHERS
P.O. BOX 280070
SAN FRANCISCO • CALIFORNIA 94128-0070

ISBN: 1-56313-808-5
TITLE #: P6808

BROWNTROUT publishes a large line of calendars, photographic books, and postcard books.
Please write for more information.

CHESAPEAKE BAY
Saxis Harbor, Virginia

BROWNTROUT PUBLISHERS • SAN FRANCISCO, CALIFORNIA

CHESAPEAKE BAY
The Chesapeake, Inner Harbor, Baltimore, Maryland

BROWNTROUT PUBLISHERS • SAN FRANCISCO, CALIFORNIA

CHESAPEAKE BAY
Eastern shore, Oxford, Maryland

BROWNTROUT PUBLISHERS • SAN FRANCISCO, CALIFORNIA

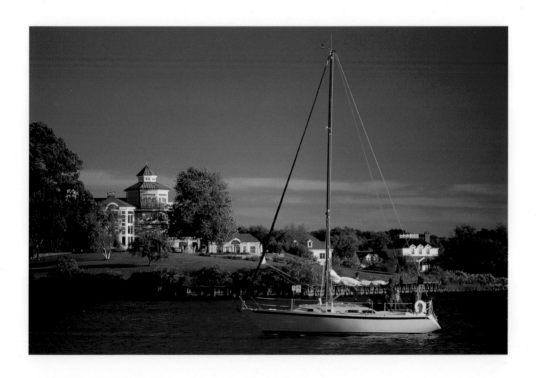

CHESAPEAKE BAY
Sailboat, Anne Arundel County, Maryland

BROWNTROUT PUBLISHERS • SAN FRANCISCO, CALIFORNIA

CHESAPEAKE BAY
Chesapeake Bay Bridge, Virginia Beach, Virginia

BROWNTROUT PUBLISHERS • SAN FRANCISCO, CALIFORNIA

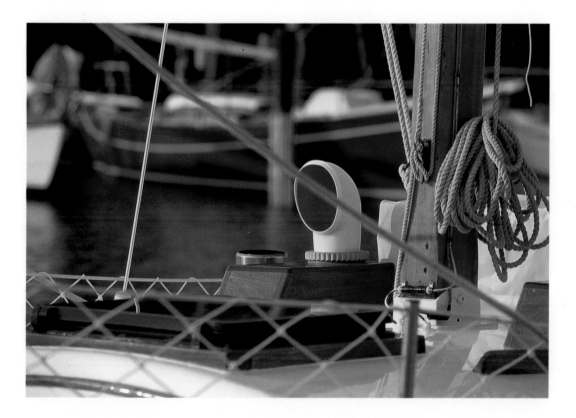

CHESAPEAKE BAY
Oxford, Maryland

BROWNTROUT PUBLISHERS • SAN FRANCISCO, CALIFORNIA

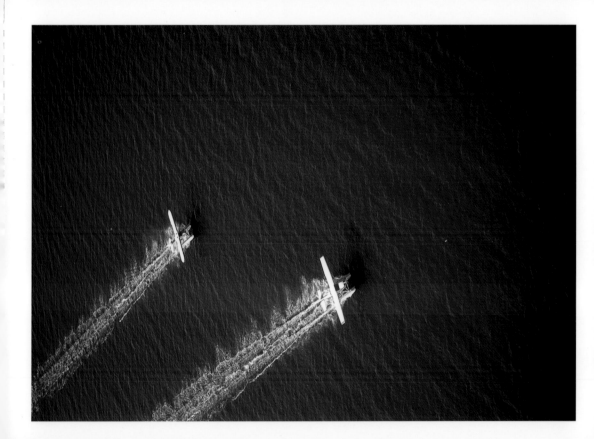

CHESAPEAKE BAY
Tandem landing of seaplanes, Middle Bay,
Stevensville, Maryland

BROWNTROUT PUBLISHERS • SAN FRANCISCO, CALIFORNIA

CHESAPEAKE BAY

Spa Creek Bridge, boats, and St. Mary's Church,
Annapolis, Maryland

BROWNTROUT PUBLISHERS • SAN FRANCISCO, CALIFORNIA

CHESAPEAKE BAY
Windsurfing, South River, Hillsmere Shores, Maryland

BROWNTROUT PUBLISHERS • SAN FRANCISCO, CALIFORNIA

CHESAPEAKE BAY
Sunset, Dominion, Maryland

BROWNTROUT PUBLISHERS • SAN FRANCISCO, CALIFORNIA

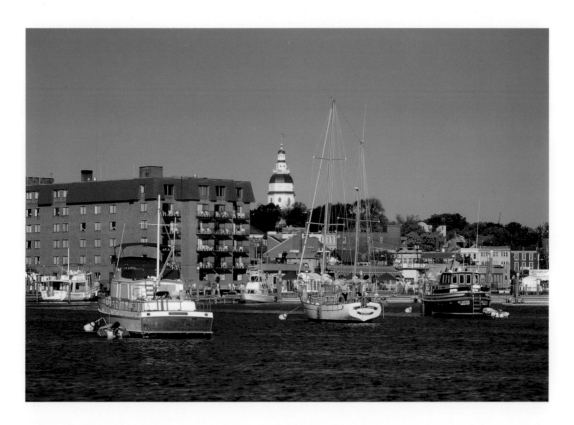

CHESAPEAKE BAY
Boats, Annapolis and State House, Maryland

BROWNTROUT PUBLISHERS • SAN FRANCISCO, CALIFORNIA

CHESAPEAKE BAY
Cape Henry Lighthouses, Ft. Story, Virginia

BROWNTROUT PUBLISHERS • SAN FRANCISCO, CALIFORNIA

CHESAPEAKE BAY
Love Point Marina and Lighthouse,
Queen Annes County, Maryland

BROWNTROUT PUBLISHERS • SAN FRANCISCO, CALIFORNIA

CHESAPEAKE BAY
Maryland Blue Crabs

BROWNTROUT PUBLISHERS • SAN FRANCISCO, CALIFORNIA

CHESAPEAKE BAY
Elliot's Island, Maryland

BROWNTROUT PUBLISHERS • SAN FRANCISCO, CALIFORNIA

CHESAPEAKE BAY
Hooper Strait Lighthouse, Chesapeake Bay Maritime Museum,
St. Michaels, Maryland

BROWNTROUT PUBLISHERS • SAN FRANCISCO, CALIFORNIA

CHESAPEAKE BAY
Hillsmere Shores Marina, Anne Arundel County, Maryland

BROWNTROUT PUBLISHERS • SAN FRANCISCO, CALIFORNIA

CHESAPEAKE BAY
Landscape from Severn Pier, Gloucester County, Virginia

BROWNTROUT PUBLISHERS • SAN FRANCISCO, CALIFORNIA

CHESAPEAKE BAY
Annapolis, Maryland

BROWNTROUT PUBLISHERS • SAN FRANCISCO, CALIFORNIA

CHESAPEAKE BAY
Pier with nets, Gloucester County, Virginia

BROWNTROUT PUBLISHERS • SAN FRANCISCO, CALIFORNIA

CHESAPEAKE BAY
Boathouse dock, Easton, Maryland

BROWNTROUT PUBLISHERS • SAN FRANCISCO, CALIFORNIA